Little KITCHEN of HORRORS

# TOMBSTONE SANDWICHES

## and Other HORRifYing LUNCHES

Ali Vega

Lerner Publications ◆ Minneapolis

Lerner Publications Company
A division of Lerner Publishing Group, Inc.
241 First Avenue North
Minneapolis, MN 55401 USA

For reading levels and more information, look up this title at www.lernerbooks.com.

Main body text set in Tw Cen MT Std.
Typeface provided by Monotype.

**Library of Congress Cataloging-in-Publication Data**

Names: Vega, Ali, author.
Title: Tombstone sandwiches and other horrifying lunches / by Ali Vega.
Description: Minneapolis : Lerner Publications, [2016] | Series: Little kitchen of horrors | Audience: Ages 7-11. | Audience: Grades 4 to 6. | Includes bibliographical references and index.
Identifiers: LCCN 2016018663 (print) | LCCN 2016020248 (ebook) | ISBN 9781512425772 (lb : alk. paper) | ISBN 9781512428070 (eb pdf)
Subjects: LCSH: Luncheons--Juvenile literature. | Cooking--Juvenile literature. | LCGFT: Cookbooks.
Classification: LCC TX735 .V44 2016 (print) | LCC TX735 (ebook) | DDC 641.5/3--dc23

LC record available at https://lccn.loc.gov/2016018663

Manufactured in the United States of America
1-41345-23289-8/30/2016

Photo Acknowledgments
The images in this book are used with the permission of: © Tomwang112/ iStockphoto, p. 4; © Mighty Media, Inc., pp. 5 (top left), 5 (top right), 5 (bottom), 9 (left), 9 (right), 10, 11 (top), 11 (middle), 11 (bottom), 12, 13 (top), 13 (bottom), 14, 15 (top), 15 (middle), 15 (bottom), 16, 17 (top), 17 (middle), 17 (bottom), 18, 19 (top), 19 (middle), 19 (bottom), 20, 21 (top), 21 (middle), 21 (bottom), 22, 23 (top), 23 (middle), 23 (bottom), 24, 25 (top), 25 (bottom), 27 (top), 27 (middle), 27 (bottom), 28, 29 (top), 29 (middle), 29 (bottom); © Elena Elisseeva/Shutterstock Images, p. 6; © IS_ImageSource/iStockphoto, p. 7; © Christopher Futcher/iStockphoto, p. 8; © David Sacks/iStockphoto, p. 30.

Front Cover: © Mighty Media, Inc.

# CONTENTS

# LOATHSOME LUNCHES

**You're home on a Saturday and hungry for lunch.** You peer into the refrigerator. Eyeballs bobbing in a bloody soup stare back at you. A pungent pile of dog doo sits on the second shelf. And look, there are leftovers! Worms writhe under hamburger-bun hats. These lunches might seem fit for a monster. But they are **edible** and even enjoyable.

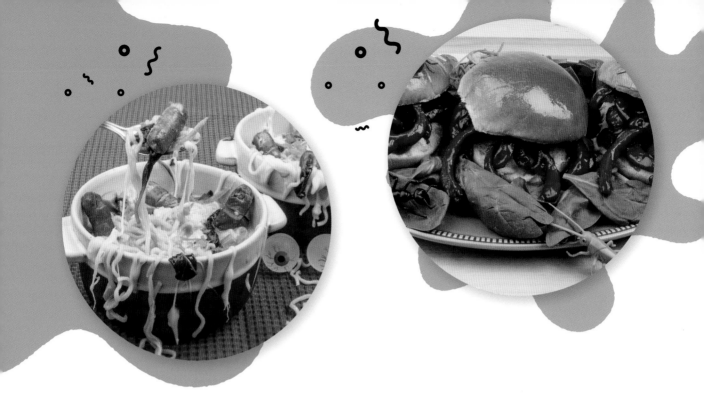

Many diners love lunches that look and sound disgusting. But revolting recipes can taste terrific. Plus, they are tons of fun to make and serve. So set the table and steel your stomach. It's time for the most sickening, vile lunches you'll ever love to eat!

# Before You
# GeT STaRTeD

**Cook Safely!** Creating revolting lunch recipes means using many different kitchen tools and appliances. These items can be very hot or sharp. Make sure to get an adult's help whenever making a recipe that requires use of an oven, stove, or knife.

**Be a Smart Chef!** Cooking gross lunches can get messy. Ask an adult for permission before starting a new cooking project. Then make sure you have a clean workspace. Wash your hands often while cooking. If you have long hair, be sure to tie it back. Make sure your guests don't have any food allergies before cooking. Adjust the recipes if you need to. Make sure your disgusting lunches are safe to eat!

## Tools You'll Need

Cooking can involve special tools and appliances. You will need the following items for these disgusting recipes:

- blender
- oven
- refrigerator
- stove or hot plate

# METRIC CONVERSION CHART

Use this handy chart to convert recipes to the metric system. If you can't find the conversion you need, ask an adult to help you find an online calculator!

| STANDARD | METRIC |
|---|---|
| ¼ teaspoon | 1.2 milliliters |
| ½ teaspoon | 2.5 ml |
| ¾ teaspoon | 3.7 ml |
| 1 teaspoon | 5 ml |
| 2 teaspoons | 10 ml |
| 1 tablespoon | 15 ml |
| ¼ cup | 59 ml |
| ⅓ cup | 79 ml |
| ½ cup | 118 ml |
| ⅔ cup | 158 ml |
| ¾ cup | 177 ml |
| 1 cup | 237 ml |

| | |
|---|---|
| 150 degrees Fahrenheit | 66 degrees Celsius |
| 300°F | 149°C |
| 350°F | 177°C |
| 400°F | 204°C |

| | |
|---|---|
| 1 ounce | 28 grams |
| 1 fluid ounce | 30 milliliters |
| 1 inch | 2.5 centimeters |
| 1 pound | 0.5 kilograms |

# GROSSIFY YOUR LUNCHES

## Nasty Names

The key to a great gross-out recipe is a truly nasty name. Once you give a lunch dish a disgusting name, it can be hard to picture it as anything else. Red sauces become blood. Dips turn into doo-doo. And hot dogs start looking a lot like severed fingers.

As you create your vile lunches, examine your ingredients. Do any inspire gag-worthy names? Make sure to announce the terrible title of each disgusting dish you serve. Your guests' looks of horror are half the fun!

# Sickening Setups

A disgusting-sounding name helps make your revolting recipes seem gross. The way you present them is also important. Think of ways to play up the foul features of each dish. Find fun props to place on the table. Fake bugs add a creepy effect. A severed prop hand can be a spooky surprise. **Sanitize** props before you use them. And be sure to remove any props from the food before actually serving it. You don't want to put your diners in danger!

# WRITHING WORM SANDWICHES

Sliced worms topped with bloody barbecue sauce make a squirming sandwich.

## Ingredients

6 hot dogs
2 tablespoons cooking oil
½ cup barbecue sauce
6 hamburger buns

**Serves: 4–6**
**Preparation Time:
10–15 minutes**

## Tools

• knife
• cutting board
• measuring spoons
• frying pan
• tongs
• mixing bowl
• measuring cups
• mixing spoon
• oven mitts

1. **Preheat** the oven to 350°F. Cut each hot dog into five or six wormlike strips.

2. With an adult's help, heat the oil in a frying pan over medium heat. Add the strips, and let them sizzle for 2 to 3 minutes.

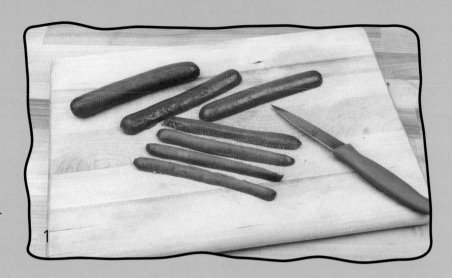

1

3. Using tongs, carefully turn each strip over. Then cook them for another 2 minutes. Repeat until the strips begin to crisp and curl. Take the hot dogs out of the frying pan and place in a bowl.

4. Cover the hot dogs with the barbecue sauce and stir.

3

5. Carefully place the buns face down directly on the oven rack. Toast for 3 minutes at 350°F. Have an adult help you remove the buns from the oven.

6. Sandwich several hot dog strips between a top and bottom bun. Repeat to make the remaining sandwiches. Watch squeamish guests squirm as they chomp on their wriggling worms!

4

# BLOOD-SOAKED EYEBALL SOUP

Creepy cheese eyeballs peer at diners from a bloody bath of tomato soup.

## Ingredients

1 sweet onion
5 tablespoons olive oil
2 **minced** garlic cloves
2½ tablespoons flour
2 teaspoons dried basil
4 cups vegetable broth
2 28-ounce cans crushed tomatoes
1 tablespoon sugar
½ teaspoon salt
½ teaspoon ground pepper
canned whole black olives
cherry-sized fresh mozzarella balls
**pimientos**

## Tools

• knife
• cutting board
• measuring spoons
• large stockpot with lid
• mixing spoon
• measuring cups
• ladle
• serving bowls

**Serves: 4–6**
**Preparation Time: 1 hour**

3

1. With an adult's help, carefully chop the onion into small pieces. Heat the oil in a stockpot over medium heat. Add the chopped onion, and cook for 5 to 7 minutes.

2. Add the garlic to the stockpot, and cook for 3 more minutes, stirring constantly. Add the flour, and stir until it is blended and not lumpy. Stir in the basil, and cook for 2 more minutes.

3. Add the vegetable broth, crushed tomatoes, sugar, salt, and pepper to the stockpot. Stir the mixture until it **simmers**. Turn the temperature to low, cover the pot, and cook for another 30 minutes.

4. Cut each olive in half. Then use a knife to carefully scoop a small hole out of each mozzarella ball. Place an olive half into the hole to make a pupil. Then add a pimiento to the center of each olive for an iris. The mozzarella balls should look like eyeballs!

5. Ladle the soup into bowls, and add two or three eyeballs to each bowl. Watch your guests enjoy a bloody bowl of warmth and comfort.

4

**TIP**

For a meatier flavor, try chicken broth instead of the vegetable broth.

# TOMBSTONE SANDWICHES

Dig up delicious grilled gravestones with these classic sandwiches!

## Ingredients

1 medium bunch kale, washed
1 tablespoon olive oil
¼ teaspoon salt
4 tablespoons butter
8 slices sourdough bread
¼ cup plus 4 teaspoons mustard
4 slices Muenster cheese
8 slices cheddar cheese
8 slices ham

## Tools

- knife
- cutting board
- large mixing bowl
- measuring spoons
- baking sheet
- oven mitts
- table knife
- frying pan with lid
- spatula
- small zipper-close plastic bag
- scissors
- serving plate

**Serves: 4**
**Preparation Time: 30-45 minutes**

1. Preheat the oven to 350°F. Cut off the kale leaves, and discard the stems. Tear the leaves into 2- to 3-inch pieces. Place the leaves in a bowl, and add the oil. Mix the kale and oil with clean hands until the leaves are completely coated. Then arrange the leaves in a single layer on a baking sheet. Sprinkle with salt. Bake the kale for 8 to 11 minutes, or until crispy.

2. Butter one side of each slice of bread. This will be the outer side. Then spread 1 teaspoon of mustard on the other side of each bread slice. Now, layer one slice of bread with one slice of Muenster, two cheddar cheese slices, and two slices of ham. Top with another slice of bread. Repeat until you have used all eight bread slices.

3. With an adult's help, heat the frying pan over medium heat. Then place one or two sandwiches in the pan. Place a lid on the pan, and cook for 3 to 4 minutes. Remove the lid, and carefully flip each sandwich. Replace the lid, and cook another 3 to 4 minutes, or until the cheese is melted and the bread is toasted. Repeat until all sandwiches are cooked.

4. Allow the sandwiches cool until they are safe to touch, and put them on a cutting board. Use a table knife to trim each sandwich into a tombstone shape.

5. Put the remaining mustard in a plastic bag. Squeeze the mustard down toward a bottom corner. Then trim off the tip of that corner. Squeeze the bag so the mustard comes out as piping. Use the piping to decorate your tombstones.

6. Arrange the crispy kale on the serving plate to look like grass. Then set up the sandwiches on the kale grass. Guests can dig into these gravestones at their own risk!

1

2

3

# SUPERSLIMY BAT WINGS

Bite into slime-soaked wings that look like they were just ripped off of bats.

## Ingredients

**Marinade**

4 tablespoons canned black beans

4 cloves minced garlic

4 tablespoons soy sauce

⅔ cup ketchup

4 tablespoons honey

2 tablespoons brown sugar

¼ cup orange juice

½ teaspoon Chinese five-spice
   powder

2 tablespoons sesame oil

blue and green food coloring

4 pounds chicken wings

## Tools

• measuring spoons

• fork

• mixing bowls, various sizes

• mixing spoon

• measuring cups

• colander

• large zipper-close plastic bags

• aluminum foil

• 2 baking sheets

• oven mitts

• serving spoon

**Serves: 4–6**
**Preparation Time: 4–5 hours
(30 minutes active)**

1. First make the **marinade**. Mash black beans with a fork in a large mixing bowl. Then stir in the garlic. Add remaining marinade ingredients to the black bean mixture, and stir to combine.

2. Add a few drops of each food coloring to the mixture, and stir until it looks greenish-black in color. Scoop out ½ cup of marinade into a small bowl, and set aside in the refrigerator.

1

3. Rinse chicken wings with water using a colander. Place the wings and marinade in a large plastic bag. Divide the wings and marinade into multiple bags if needed. Seal each bag, and make sure the top is closed tightly before shaking it to coat the wings in the marinade.

4. Place the bag in the refrigerator, and let it sit for 3 or more hours.

5. Preheat the oven to 325°F. Put a sheet of aluminum foil on each baking sheet. Arrange the wings on the foil.

3

6. Bake the wings for 45 minutes to 1 hour. Then serve to your guests with a spoonful of extra marinade for each wing. These beastly bat wings will be so tasty, they will fly off the plates!

5

TIP

Chinese five-spice powder is a blend of cinnamon, cloves, fennel, star anise, and peppercorns. It can be purchased at most grocery stores.

# MAGGOT AND BUG SALAD

This creepy-crawly salad will have diners itching to take their first bites.

## Ingredients

½ red onion
1 16-ounce can white beans
1 6.5-ounce can marinated
    artichoke hearts

### Dressing

1 clove minced garlic
2 tablespoons olive oil
1 tablespoon lemon juice
½ teaspoon dried oregano
½ teaspoon lemon pepper
¼ teaspoon salt

1½ cups uncooked orzo pasta
1 cup crumbled feta cheese
15–20 cherry tomatoes
1 16-ounce can whole black olives

## Tools

• knife
• cutting board
• large serving bowl
• measuring spoons
• mixing spoon
• large stockpot
• measuring cups
• colander

**Serves: 4**
**Preparation Time: 1 hour, 30 minutes**

1. Carefully chop the onion into ½-inch pieces. Combine the onion, beans, artichoke hearts and their juices, and dressing ingredients into a large bowl. Stir together, and refrigerate for 1 hour.

2. Fill a stockpot with water, and bring to a **boil** over high heat with an adult's help. Add the orzo pasta and cook for 8 to 10 minutes. Carefully drain the pasta using a colander. Set it aside to cool.

3. Add the cooled pasta to the bean mixture, and stir to combine. Stir in the feta cheese.

4. Cut the cherry tomatoes in half the long way. Then cut each half down the middle one more time, stopping just before you reach the top. The tomato should look like a bug's wings!

5. Cut each olive in half the long way. Then cut it in half the long way again. The olives should look like small beetles.

6. Arrange the tomato and olive bugs so they look like they are crawling out of the salad. Then serve this squirming salad to your bug-eyed guests!

1

3

4

# MONSTER-SNOT RAMEN

**Slurp up the finger boogers in this slimy ramen!**

## Ingredients

4 ounces white mushrooms
1 tablespoon sesame oil
4 cloves minced garlic
1 tablespoon freshly grated ginger
4 cups chicken broth
¼ cup soy sauce
3 3-ounce packages dried ramen noodles (don't use the seasoning packet)
1 grated carrot
3 cups fresh spinach
8–10 mini hot dogs
½ cup shredded white cheese
2 teaspoons chopped green onions

## Tools

- knife
- cutting board
- large stockpot
- grater
- measuring spoons
- mixing spoon
- measuring cups
- medium saucepan
- colander
- ladle
- serving bowls
- fork

**Serves: 4**
**Preparation Time: 20–30 minutes**

1. Carefully chop the mushrooms into quarters. With an adult's help, heat the oil in a stockpot over medium heat. Add the garlic and ginger, and cook for 1 to 3 minutes, stirring constantly. Stir in the chicken broth, mushrooms, soy sauce, and 3 cups of water. Bring the mixture to a boil over high heat, and then reduce the temperature to medium-low.

1

2. Let the mixture simmer for 10 minutes. Add in the ramen noodles and cook for 2 to 3 minutes.

3. Add the carrot and spinach. Cook for 2 more minutes and remove from heat.

3

4. Fill a saucepan with water, and bring it to a boil over high heat with an adult's help. Meanwhile, shape the hot dog fingers. Use a knife to carefully carve a fingernail into the end of each hot dog. Then make three or four slits halfway down each hot dog to look like knuckles. Boil the hot dogs in the saucepan for 3 to 4 minutes. Remove from heat. Then drain using a colander.

5. Ladle the ramen soup into individual serving bowls. Add a bit of cheese to each bowl. As the cheese melts, swirl it around with a fork to make it look like runny snot.

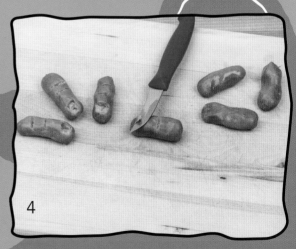
4

6. Add two or three hot dogs to each bowl and **garnish** with the green onions. Then watch your guests relish this revolting ramen.

TIP

If you don't have dried ramen noodles, try using 1 pound of spaghetti noodles instead. Cook the noodles according to the package directions.

# MUDDY EARTHWORM SPAGHETTI

Chow down on a muddy mass of worms as they navigate a plate of dirt!

## Ingredients

2 15-ounce cans black beans

**Sauce**

2 cups barbecue sauce

1 tablespoon Worcestershire sauce

1 9-ounce jar red pepper jelly

2 tablespoons honey

2 tablespoons brown sugar

1 teaspoon red pepper flakes

1 1-pound package spaghetti

## Tools

- knife
- cutting board
- medium saucepan
- measuring cups
- measuring spoons
- mixing spoon
- large stockpot
- colander
- serving plates

**Serves: 4**
**Preparation Time: 35–40 minutes**

If you don't have red pepper jelly, you can substitute seedless raspberry jam.

1

1. Drain the beans. Then carefully chop them into small, crumbly pieces to look like dirt.

2. Add all the sauce ingredients to a saucepan. Stir to combine. Warm the sauce on a medium-low setting for 10 to 15 minutes. Then reduce the heat to low until you are ready to use it.

2

3. Fill a stockpot three-quarters full with water. With an adult's help, bring the water to a boil over high heat. Add the spaghetti, and cook according to the package directions.

4. Carefully drain the spaghetti through a colander. Put the spaghetti back in the stockpot.

5. Gently stir the chopped beans into the spaghetti. Then add the sauce, and gently stir to combine.

5

6. Scoop the earthy mixture onto plates. Warn your guests to stab any slimy stragglers that try to escape!

# DOG PILE ON RICE

**No doo-doo bags needed for this tasty pile of chili and rice!**

## Ingredients

### Chili

3 tablespoons olive oil

1 onion chopped into ¼-inch pieces

1 pound ground turkey

½ teaspoon dried basil

1 teaspoon ground cumin

1 teaspoon dried oregano

2 tablespoons chili powder

1 teaspoons salt

1 tablespoon of flour

1 6-ounce can of tomato paste

2 15-ounce cans chopped
   tomatoes, drained

1 15-ounce can kidney beans,
   drained

3 cups spinach leaves

**Serves: 6**
**Preparation Time:**
**2–4 hours**

### Green Rice

½ cup cilantro

1 cup spinach leaves

1¼ cup chicken broth

1 minced garlic clove

1 teaspoon salt

2 tablespoons butter

1½ cups long-grain white rice

## Tools

• measuring spoons

• large stockpot with lid

• knife

• cutting board

• mixing spoon

• blender

• medium saucepan with lid

• serving plate

• large zipper-close plastic bag

• scissors

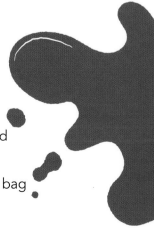

1. To make the chili, heat 3 tablespoons of oil in a stockpot over medium heat with an adult's help. Add the chopped onion, and cook until **translucent**. Add the ground turkey, and cook until browned. Add the basil, cumin, oregano, chili powder, salt, flour, and tomato paste. Stir together, and cook for 5 minutes. Add the tomatoes, beans, and 3 cups of spinach leaves. Cover and simmer for 1 hour on low heat.

2. While the chili cooks, make the green rice. Blend cilantro, 1 cup of spinach leaves, chicken broth, 1¼ cup water, garlic, and salt in a blender.

3. Melt the butter in a saucepan over medium heat. Add the uncooked rice, and stir for 1 minute.

4. Pour the blender ingredients into the saucepan. Then turn heat up to high and bring to a boil. Turn the heat down to very low. Cover the saucepan, and cook for 30 minutes. Remove the pan from heat, keeping it covered, and set aside.

5. Take the chili off the heat, and let it cool. Transfer as much chili as will fit to the clean blender. Blend the chili in batches until it is smooth.

6. Scoop some of the green rice onto a serving plate. Then pour 1 cup of the chili into a plastic bag. Clip off one corner of the bag to make a hole. Squeeze a few chili droppings onto a bed of green rice. Provide guests with the proper utensils for pickup, then present your tasty poo piles!

**TIP**

If needed, **reinforce** the corner of the plastic bag with duct tape.

# CREATURE-IN-MY-POT PIE

Take a bite of this creeping creature before it takes a bite out of you!

## Ingredients

3 pounds boneless, skinless chicken pieces
6 tablespoons butter
salt
pepper
1 large onion
3 carrots
3 celery stalks
½ cup all-purpose flour
2½ cups chicken stock
1½ cups milk
1 teaspoon dried thyme leaves
¾ cup green peas, frozen or fresh
2 teaspoons dried parsley
2 8-ounce tubes refrigerated crescent roll dough
pimientos and almond slices (optional for decorating)

## Tools

- large zipper-close plastic bag
- rolling pin
- measuring spoons
- frying pan
- tongs
- knife
- cutting board
- large stockpot
- measuring cups
- mixing spoon
- **whisk**
- pizza cutter
- 4 oven-safe bowls and plates
- ladle
- 1–2 baking sheets
- oven mitts

**Serves: 4**
**Preparation Time: 1 hour, 30 minutes**

1. Rinse the chicken pieces in water. Then place as many as will fit in a plastic bag. Use the rolling pin to roll the pieces out until they are the same thickness. Repeat until all the chicken is rolled out.

2. With an adult's help, heat 2 tablespoons of butter in a frying pan over medium-high heat. Add a few shakes of salt and pepper. Cook the chicken pieces for 5 to 8 minutes on one side. Turn the chicken over, and cook on the other side for 5 to 8 minutes. Turn over once more, and cook another 5 to 8 minutes or until done. Remove the chicken from heat, and let it cool. When cool, cut the chicken into bite-size pieces.

3. Chop the onion, carrots, and celery into ½-inch pieces on a clean cutting board.

4. In a stockpot, melt the remaining butter over medium heat. Add the onion, carrots, and celery. Then cook for 10 to 12 minutes.

5. Add the flour. Cook for 1 to 2 minutes, stirring constantly. Make sure all flour lumps disappear. Using a whisk, stir in the chicken stock. Next add the milk, and reduce the temperature to low. Simmer for 10 minutes, whisking often.

6. Add the cooked chicken pieces, thyme, peas, parsley, and ½ teaspoon each of salt and pepper. Stir to combine, and keep on low heat while you prepare the crust.

Creature-in-My-Pot Pie
*continued next page*

**TIP**

Fresh herbs can add fantastic flavor to any dish. Substitute any of the dried herbs for fresh ones to really impress your guests!

7

*Creature-in-My-Pot Pie, continued*

7 Preheat the oven to 325°F. Unroll the first crescent roll dough onto a large, clean cutting board. Use a pizza cutter to cut the dough into several small strips. Unroll the second dough and cut into four equal pieces. Shape these into four flattened circles to look like heads.

8

8 Place four oven-safe serving bowls on four oven-safe plates. Then ladle the filling into the bowls.

9 Place a dough strip inside the first bowl, and trail it down the outside to attach to the plate. Arrange several more strips around the bowl. Place a round piece of dough on top of the bowl to look like a head.

9

10 Repeat step 9 until all the bowls are decorated. Then put the plates on one or two baking sheets, depending on how much space you need. Bake for 12 to 15 minutes, or until lightly browned.

11 Wearing oven mitts, carefully remove the baking sheet from the oven and allow to cool for 7 to 10 minutes. If you like, make a face out of pimientos and almond slices. Then serve these creepy creatures to hungry guests. Remember to warn them that the bowls and plates will be hot!

# WRAPPING UP

## Cleaning Up

Once you are done cooking, it is time to clean up! Make sure to wipe up spills, wash dishes, and clear the table. Wash and put away any props you used that don't belong in the kitchen. Make sure any leftovers are properly packaged and refrigerated.

## Keep Cooking!

Get inspired by your loathsome lunch creations. Think of other dishes and ingredients that might look terrifying but taste terrific. Or go back and make your own versions of the revolting recipes you tried. Think disgusting, and keep on cooking!

# GLOSSARY

**boil:** liquid that has become so hot that bubbles form and rise to the top

**edible:** something that can be safely eaten

**garnish:** to decorate food before serving it

**marinade:** a sauce in which food is soaked to make it more flavorful

**minced:** chopped or cut into very small pieces

**pimientos:** sweet peppers that are often chopped into small pieces and stuffed into olives

**preheat:** to heat an oven to the required temperature before putting in the food

**reinforce:** to strengthen something by adding more material

**sanitize:** to clean something so that it is free of germs

**simmers:** when a heated liquid is not quite boiling and has very small bubbles

**translucent:** almost clear

**whisk:** to stir very quickly using a fork or a tool made of curved wire, also called a whisk

# FURTHER INFORMATION

**Hammer, Melinda. *Kid Chef: The Foodie Kids Cookbook.*** Berkley, CA: Sonoma Press, 2016.
Practice your cooking skills with this cookbook full of tasty recipes and tips for budding chefs.

**Larsen, Jennifer S. *Tasty Sandwiches.*** Minneapolis: Millbrook Press, 2013.
Learn how to make even more delicious lunch recipes to wow your family and friends.

**Lunch: Super Healthy Kids**
http://www.superhealthykids.com/recipe-category/lunch/
Come up with creative way to spookify these healthful lunch recipes.

**Thirteen Easy Halloween Lunch Ideas**
http://www.momables.com/13-easy-halloween-lunch-ideas/
These simple recipes are perfect or Halloween or anytime you want to gross out lunch guests.

# INDEX